SPIKE LEE

Filmmaker

—PEOPLE TO KNOW—

SPIKE LEE

Filmmaker

Bob Bernotas

ENSLOW PUBLISHERS, INC.

Bloy St. and Ramsey Ave.   P.O. Box 38
Box 777   Aldershot
Hillside, N.J. 07205   Hants GU12 6BP
U.S.A.   U.K.

Library of Congress Cataloging-in-Publication Data

Bernotas, Bob.
     Spike Lee : filmmaker / Bob Bernotas
        p. cm. — (People to know)
     Filmography: p.
     Includes bibliographical references (p.   ) and index.
     Summary: A biography of the African-American filmmaker Spike Lee,
from his childhood in New York through his days as the controversial
director of such films as "Malcolm X."
     ISBN 0-89490-416-7
     1. Lee, Spike—Juvenile literature. 2. Motion picture producers
and directors—United States—Biography—Juvenile literature.
[1. Lee, Spike. 2. Motion picture producers and directors. 3. Afro-
Americans—Biography.] I. Title. II. Series.
PN1998.3.L44B47   1993
791.43'0233'092—dc20
   [B]   92-41234
                                             CIP
                                           AC

Printed in the United States of America

10 9 8 7 6 5 4 3 2 1

Contents

Spike Lee

1

Controversy at Cannes

The place: the annual Film Festival in Cannes, France. The time: morning, May 19, 1989. A new film was being premiered for the press. When the screening ended, the assembled reporters and critics left the room. Many were dismayed, some were awed, but all were talking—even arguing—about the remarkable motion picture they had just seen.

According to a report in *Rolling Stone* magazine, *USA Today*'s columnist Jeannie Williams was frightened by what she saw. "I live in New York!" she exclaimed. "I don't need this movie in New York this summer!" However, the new picture thrilled Roger Ebert, the film critic of the *Chicago Sun-Times.* "It's a great film, a great film," he declared. "If this doesn't win the grand prize, I'm not coming back next year."[1]

The film they were talking about was *Do the Right Thing*, which was written, directed, and produced by a thirty-two-year-old African-American filmmaker named Spike Lee. This was not Lee's first trip to the Cannes festival. Three years before, he went there to show his first feature film, the acclaimed *She's Gotta Have It*. Back then he had to share a cramped rented apartment with seven other people.

Now, with two successful movies under his belt, and a big-budget film having its premiere here, Lee was staying in a two-room suite at the Carlton that was paid for by Universal Pictures. But despite these posh surroundings, he still could be found strolling around the hotel in his usual attire—sneakers, jeans, T-shirt, Public Enemy medallion, baseball cap, and New York Knicks windbreaker.

Do the Right Thing takes place in Bedford-Stuyvesant, a largely black section of Brooklyn, on the hottest day of a hot summer. Racial tensions are high. At the end of this long day, the tensions finally erupt into a shocking and violent climax. A young African-American man is killed by the police. In retaliation, the people in the neighborhood burn down a white-owned pizzeria.

The next morning, after the death and destruction, nothing is resolved. As the film ends a pair of quotations appear on the screen. The first one, by Dr. Martin Luther King, Jr., preaches nonviolence in the face of bigotry. The second one, by Malcolm X, argues that

African-American people have the right to defend themselves whenever they are attacked. The statements are punctuated with a picture of the two leaders standing side by side.

The film ends on an intentionally ambiguous note. What is "the right thing?" The movie never says. The audience members must answer this question for themselves.

At the press conference that followed the screening, Lee was at his best—feisty, articulate, and self-confident. The reporters and critics bombarded him with questions. He answered each one in his typically direct manner.

One journalist noted that racial tension already was on the increase in New York and wondered what effect this film might have when it was released there at the end of June. In other words, would *Do the Right Thing* incite people to violence? "It'll probably be hot again this summer," Lee responded, "and if anything happens this summer it won't be because of this film. It will be because cops kill somebody else for no reason."

He added, however, "This film is not about New York City, this film is about the world. . . . Racism is all over the world."[2]

Another writer wondered why a movie that took place in an African-American ghetto did not show anyone using drugs. "This film is not about drugs," Lee replied sharply. "It's about people and racism."[3] He found the question offensive—racist—and said so.

"The minute we have a black film that takes place in the ghetto," he complained, "people want to know where the drugs are . . . because that's the way you think of black people."[4] A white filmmaker would not have been asked this question, he believed. "How many journalists who saw *Working Girl* or *Rain Man*," he wondered, "questioned where are the drugs? Nobody."[5]

He also was asked about those two quotes that were placed side by side at the film's end, the statements from Martin Luther King, Jr. and Malcolm X. Reporters wanted to know which view Lee agreed with—nonviolence or self-defense.

"In certain times," he explained, "both philosophies can be appropriate, but in this day and age . . . I'm leaning more toward the philosophies of Malcolm X. . . . When you're being hit upside the head with a brick, I don't think young black America is just going to turn the other cheek."[6]

Naturally, a reporter asked him, "What is 'the right thing'?" It was a loaded question. The whole point of his film was that people had to work through this question for themselves and discover their *own* answers. "I don't know," Lee responded. "I know what the *wrong* thing is: racism."[7]

For someone else, this barrage of questions might have been an ordeal. Lee, however, relished the attention and he welcomed the controversy that his film prompted. To him, it was a signal that *Do the Right*

Thing could get people arguing, debating, *thinking*. Lee has always understood the value of publicity. A little bit of controversy can be good for the box office.

Unfortunately, the controversy did not sit well with the festival's judges. Four days later, the awards were announced. Not only did *Do the Right Thing* fail to win the coveted grand prize, the *Palme d'Or,* it was shut out of the awards completely. Lee was disappointed. "We got robbed," he told reporters.[8]

He decided to put this setback behind him. In a little over a month, the film would open in theaters all over the United States. Judging from the uproar Lee and his film caused at Cannes, he knew there would be an even greater storm ahead. But he would be ready for it.

2

Growing Up

Spike Lee keeps a book that he treasures—*Fallen Prince,*
by Donald E. Stone—in the desk in his office at Forty
Acres and a Mule Filmworks. It begins with the story of
Mike and Phoebe, two African slaves. They lived on
different plantations in South Carolina before the Civil
War.

Mike and Phoebe were "married" on Christmas Day,
1811. They had seven children and one more was on the
way. Then Phoebe's master decided to move to Alabama,
and it seemed that they would be separated forever.

Mike's master told him that he could buy his
freedom—for $1,900. Every night, after his duties on
the plantation were done, Mike worked hard, but he
earned only a pittance. It took many years, but he finally
had enough money to become free. He set out in search

of Phoebe, and found her in a slave cabin in Snow Hill, Alabama, in May of 1825. They remained together until Phoebe died in 1864.

Their fourth child, James Carmichael, had a daughter, Martha Carmichael Edwards. She had a son, William James Edwards, a sickly baby whom nobody thought would live.

Willie did live, although no one believed that this crippled, stuttering boy would amount to much. But he had a dream. There was a school for young African-American men and women, Tuskegee Institute in Tuskegee, Alabama, and he wanted to go there. Willie worked long and hard to earn the $8-a-month tuition. He enrolled in Tuskegee in 1889.

Four years later, Edwards graduated with honors. He had become a protegé of Booker T. Washington, the school's founder and renowned African-American educator. In 1893, the year he left Tuskegee, Edwards established the Snow Hill Institute in Snow Hill, Alabama. It grew into one of the finest schools of its kind.

William James Edwards was the great-grandfather of Spike Lee. His struggles and triumphs—and those of Mike and Phoebe—are the family heritage. Hard work and the refusal to quit, even when things look dark, are family traditions. Lee gets inspiration from these courageous ancestors.

Shelton Jackson Lee was born in Atlanta, Georgia,

on March 20, 1957. He was the oldest of five children. His mother, Jacquelyn Lee, nicknamed the child "Spike," but no one really remembers why. "I guess she thought I was a tough baby," Lee joked to *People* magazine.[1] "I never liked it," Spike's grandmother, Zimmie Shelton, complains.[2]

When Spike was two years old, the family moved to New York City so that his father, jazz bassist Bill Lee, could, in his words, "be around great artists." Spike grew up in the borough of Brooklyn, where he still lives. Times were often hard for the Lee family. "We weren't starving," Lee recalls, "but sometimes it was hand-to-mouth."[3]

Bill Lee always preferred the pure sound of the so-called "stand-up," or acoustic, bass. He never liked the more popular electric Fender bass and simply refused to play it. If he had taken up the electric bass, Bill Lee could have gotten more work. Making ends meet would have been easier. But his integrity as an artist was more important to him than money. In the long run, he believes that the struggle was worth it. "I have been well rewarded for my convictions," Bill Lee says. He feels that his children "are the benefit of my hard work and will be dedicated to the truth."[4]

Spike's mother, Jacquelyn Lee, taught art and literature at St. Ann's School in Brooklyn Heights. She was the disciplinarian of the Lee household. "My father," Lee told film critic Roger Ebert, "whatever you wanted

Spike Lee's childhood home in Brooklyn, New York.

to do, he would just say it was OK. He was a great father, but his way of discipline was to have none. My mother knew better. She was the heavy, but she had to take that role, or we'd have had no parental supervision at all."[5]

In Lee's view, the most valuable gift that Bill and Jacquelyn Lee gave their children was a love for culture, especially African-American culture. "We had great exposure to [the] arts at a young age," Lee notes with pride. "My mother liked the theater and liked music. My father is a jazz musician so music was always being played in the house."[6]

From the time he was five years old, Spike was going to movies and Broadway shows with his mother. She also brought the family to exhibits by African-American artists and gave them books by African-American writers. Bill Lee often took his children to nightclubs and festivals, where he backed up artists like folk singer Odetta and the legendary jazz trumpeter, Miles Davis. It is very important for young people to experience the arts, Lee believes. "If you're not exposed as a child," he insists, "it's a serious setback."[7]

Jacquelyn and Bill Lee did encourage their children to love the arts, but they never pushed Spike or his siblings into any particular field. Spike did take piano and guitar lessons for a brief time, but soon lost interest in them. "I did not want to be a musician," he recalls, "and my parents, luckily, did not press me and my brothers and sister to be musicians."[8]

Sports were young Spike's number one love. He was always organizing games in the neighborhood and mailing out baseball cards to be autographed by his favorite players. He often had to fight with his sister Joie to watch New York Knicks basketball games on TV when she wanted to see *The Brady Bunch.* "Growing up," he notes, "I wanted to be an athlete. The sport didn't matter; it just depended on what season it was: basketball, baseball, football—I played 'em all."[9]

However, Spike's size was never as big as his desire. He did not grow up to be a great sports hero, but he is still a great sports fan. He goes to New York Mets baseball games and New York Giants football games whenever he can. Whenever the Knicks are playing in Madison Square Garden, there's a very good chance that Lee will be there, sitting courtside, high-fiving the players.

Besides his only sister, Joie, Lee has three brothers—Chris, David, and Cinque. The oldest in the family, Spike enjoyed teasing his younger brothers and sister. "Spike used to get weird things in his head," Joie Lee remembers. "For a while, he decided David had a crush on Annette Funicello," who was the star of many teen-oriented beach movies of the 1960s.

"David hardly knew who Annette Funicello *was*," she continues, "but Spike kept saying, 'David, you know that you love Annette.'" David Lee, not surprisingly, does not like to admit that this ever happened. "I don't remember that," he claims.[10]

Spike's quick wit was good for more than just teasing his siblings. As one of the smallest boys in his class, Spike sometimes found himself in tense situations. Once, two bigger boys decided they were going to beat him up. They warned him that they would see him after school. Thinking fast, Spike talked his teacher into letting him go home early that day.

Perhaps because he was small as a child, Lee grew up somewhat suspicious, even withdrawn. "He was probably never the most popular guy in class," says his friend, musician Branford Marsalis.[11] He is uncomfortable around people he does not know. He gives interviews only reluctantly, and he often seems bored by the interviewer's questions.

Spike Lee is just 5 feet, 6 inches tall and weighs, in his words, "a solid 120 pounds."[12] In his father's view, Lee's small stature may have helped spur him on to a successful career in films. "I think Spike's size has had a lot to do with his determination to do something big," Bill Lee says.[13]

But certain childhood experiences also may have influenced Lee's drive to "do something big." From 1963 to 1965, beginning when Spike was six years old, the Lee family spent the summer with relatives in Alabama. There he encountered the kinds of open racial discrimination that were common then in the South. He remembers being bothered by such things as separate bathrooms and drinking fountains for white and black people.

Lee also experienced racial bigotry growing up in the North. When his family moved into a white neighborhood in Brooklyn, he remembers being called racist names. "People always think discrimination is just in the South. But it's like Malcolm X said," Lee observes, quoting the militant black leader who is the subject of his sixth film, " 'The South begins at the Canadian border.' "[14] These childhood experiences remain etched in Lee's memory, and have influenced his work as a filmmaker.

African-American culture and identity are recurring themes in Spike Lee's work. Even when he was growing up, it was important to Spike that he have a strong sense of himself as a black person. Because Jacquelyn Lee was a teacher at St. Ann's School, her children could have gone there for free. St. Ann's was largely white, however. Spike wanted to be with other African-American students, so he chose to attend a public school in his neighborhood.

Chris joined his older brother in public school, but David, Joie, and Cinque decided to go to St. Ann's. "Spike used to point out the differences in the schooling," Joie Lee notes, "the differences in our friends, that all the people I knew were white."[15]

In one key way, it seems, going to these different schools may have influenced the Lee children's lives. When it came time for college, David enrolled in the elite Yale University and Joie went to another predominantly white school, Sarah Lawrence College. Spike, however, had taken a different route when he graduated high school. In 1975, he decided to attend Morehouse College in Atlanta, Georgia, the alma mater of his father and his grandfather—a *black* school.

3

"Born to Be a Filmmaker"

Founded in 1867, Morehouse College in Atlanta, Georgia, is a respected, highly selective place of higher learning. One of its most famous and distinguished alumni was the Rev. Dr. Martin Luther King, Jr. Bill Lee was one of his classmates.

The eighteen-year-old Spike Lee arrived at Morehouse in the fall of 1975. It was, he felt, a natural step for him to take. "My father and my grandfather, they went to college, so it was there for me, too. I never thought about rebelling," he told an interviewer, "not going to college. It was what I was going to do."[1]

Like many college freshmen, Lee at first was undecided about his plans for the future. For many students, the first year or two of college is a time to experiment and explore, to look around and try to find subjects that interest them, before they finally settle into a program of study.

From the time he was a child, his parents had taken him to shows, concerts, and exhibitions, so Lee had a strong interest in the arts. In his sophomore year, he began to "dib and dab,"[2] as he puts it, with a super-8 movie camera. He decided to major in mass communications at Morehouse and made, he recalls, "one or two" films.

"That's where I had my appetite whet," he remembers. "That's where I became interested in film and that's where I decided I wanted to become a filmmaker."[3]

In Lee's junior year, his mother suddenly became ill with liver cancer. He rushed home from school to see her. It would be for the last time—two days after her son returned to Morehouse, Jacquelyn Lee died. Lee often thinks about his mother, and he gets much of his inspiration from her. "I take the fruits of her labors for my strength and fortitude," he said. "My only regret is that she did not live to see my films."[4]

Every year Morehouse, like many colleges, holds a homecoming weekend when past graduates revisit their old campus. The highlight of the Morehouse homecoming is the coronation pageant, the lavish ceremony and festivities that accompany the crowning of the "homecoming queen."

In his senior year, Lee was chosen to direct the

pageant. It was, he believes, an important opportunity for him. "You supervise hundreds of people," he explains. "That's where I really started to learn my organization skills."[5] A filmmaker must know how to handle a large cast and crew, and directing the Morehouse pageant provided Lee with some valuable firsthand experience.

As the pageant director, Lee showed the same kind of independent vision that he now employs as a filmmaker. He felt that the coronation pageant should be like the old 1940s Hollywood musicals that fascinated him when he was a child. He insisted that the women be dressed in elegant, floor-length gowns instead of the usual slinky, somewhat revealing, dresses that they normally wore for the pageant. A group of male students heard about his plans and actually threatened to beat him up—they wanted to see pretty women in slinky dresses. Lee, however, stood his ground and in the end they did it his way.

Lee looks back on his years at Morehouse with a mixture of fondness and amusement. "I'm glad I went there," he told *Essence* magazine, "but I was always an outsider, a rebel." He feels that you should always strive to assert your own identity. This refusal to conform is one of his most important characteristics as a filmmaker.

He also exhibited this trait in college. "There's a certain image of a Morehouse man," he continued, "squeaky-clean, always in a suit and tie, a business major, in a fraternity. . . . That just wasn't me."[6] College student or successful filmmaker, Spike Lee always has insisted on being "me."

There was one thing about Morehouse that really bothered Lee. He observed how some of the lighter-skinned students looked down on their darker-skinned classmates. This sort of color bias among African-American people, Lee feels, is reflected in the society at large. "The people with the money," he laments, "most of them have light skin. They have the Porsches, the BMW's, the quote good hair unquote. When I was in school, we saw all this going on. I remember saying, 'Some of this stuff has to be in a movie.'"[7] Someday it would be.

But Lee needed some training in the art and craft of filmmaking before he could begin putting his ambitious ideas on the screen. After he graduated from Morehouse in 1979, he enrolled in the master's degree program at New York University's prestigious film school. He paid for his tuition with money he earned by cleaning film at a movie distribution company.

Lee's years at NYU were turbulent. His first-year project was a short film, *The Answer*. It was about a young African-American screen writer hired to work on a remake of the classic silent movie, *Birth of a Nation*, directed by D. W. Griffith. In terms of filmmaking technique, *Birth of a Nation* was one of the most influential motion pictures in history. However, it also

24

contained many racist messages and stereotypes. Lee wanted to highlight the dilemmas that this project would create for a black filmmaker.

His professors were not pleased with his work. Lee suspects that they didn't like him criticizing a revered film pioneer like Griffith. However, the school's program director insists that his idea was too ambitious for a twenty-minute film, and that it was badly executed. But whatever the reason, Lee notes, "I was told that I was whiskers away from being kicked out."[8] But he managed to survive this crisis and stay in the program.

In 1982, his final year at NYU, he submitted his master's thesis, an hour-long film called *Joe's Bed-Stuy Barbershop: We Cut Heads*. This story of a barber in a black Brooklyn neighborhood who gets into trouble with gangsters created a sensation. Lee won a student Academy Award. The film was screened at the Museum of Modern Art in New York as part of the 1983 New Directors/New Films Festival. Every year this festival showcases the best new independent works. The film was also broadcast during 1983 and 1984 on public television stations throughout the country.

After graduating from the NYU Film School, Lee took a $200-a-week job at a movie distribution house cleaning and shipping film, while he tried to line up his first professional project. Some major talent agencies were interested in him because of *Joe's Bed-Stuy Barbershop*. But, Lee recalls, "they were unable to generate me any work . . . so that just cemented in my mind what I always thought all along: that I would have to go out and do it alone, not rely on anyone else."[9]

He began working on the script for what was supposed to be his first feature film. It was called *Messenger,* and it was about a bicycle messenger who has to become the head of his family when his mother dies suddenly. The script was finished by the summer of 1984. Lee hired a crew, cast the film, and was all ready to start shooting. He even had *Messenger* T-shirts. The only thing he didn't have was enough money.

Lee wanted to pay his actors the same rate that actors get when they appear in small-budget experimental films. This would cost him less money. However, the Screen Actors Guild, which is the union that represents movie performers, felt that the film was "too commercial." It insisted that he pay the standard wage. Lee managed to obtain small grants from the New York State Council on the Arts and the American Film Institute, but he needed more money. His producer promised that he could raise the rest of the capital, but he never came through. Lee waited all summer. Finally he had to pull the plug on *Messenger* before even a single frame was shot.

Friends and family had put money into Lee's doomed project. Professional actors and technicians had signed on with him and then watched the film self-destruct. "It was hard for me to face people," he wrote later, "folks were mad as hell; and they had a right to be because they had lost money and had turned down *real jobs, real employment,* to work on a nonexistent film."[10] Lee was devastated and ashamed.

Once the initial shock and disappointment wore off, Lee began to do some serious thinking about this failure. In his mind he rehashed what had happened, and he tried to discover what he had done wrong. "I had committed the cardinal sin of young filmmakers," he concluded. "I was in over my head. Everything—the budget, the size, the scope—was too big."[11] And so *Messenger* proved to be an important learning experience for Spike Lee, and a real turning point in his budding career.

Next time Lee would not be so ambitious. "I swore on my mother's grave that I would never commit the errors I'd made on *Messenger* again and that the next summer, the summer of 1985, I would be back."[12] He began work on a new script that this time, he felt, was "do-able"—a simple story with just a few characters and no sets.

That following summer, Lee, true to his word, started shooting on his first feature film. He had his share of problems on this project as well. Still, having survived the *Messenger* fiasco, Lee now felt stronger, more determined, and better able to cope with whatever setbacks he encountered along the way.

It was as if he were on a mission. He had a vision, a

message, and he would get it out no matter what. Many times while working on the new film, things began to look bleak. Money would grow short, bills would pile up, creditors would demand to be paid. "It's been killing me," Lee would write in his diary. "I will, however, never quit. I was born to be a filmmaker."[13]

4

"None of My Movies Are Comedies"

The movie screen went dark, the lights came on, and a serious young man spoke to the small, invited audience. "I'm Spike Lee," he announced in a low-key, sincere manner, "and I hope that you liked the film, and I'll be calling you soon about becoming financially involved in helping us complete it."[1]

This scene took place often during the second half of 1985. Lee would show potential investors a partially completed rough cut of *She's Gotta Have It*, his new movie-in-progress. Maybe they would give him the money he needed to finish it.

Lee got the idea for this film when he heard some of his male friends bragging about how many girlfriends they had. Most of them, he noticed, believed in a double standard. "If word gets back to them," Lee muses, "that one of those women is not even seeing another man, but just thinking about it, they go through the roof."[2] He decided to make a movie that would turn the tables on these individuals.

Lee came up with a questionnaire about the dating habits of young women. He called up about thirty female friends and asked them to answer it. The responses to his informal survey became the basis for *She's Gotta Have It*.

The central character of the film, Nola Darling, has three boyfriends. But, Lee insists, "Nola is not sneaky or dishonest in the relationships. The three men all know about each other."[3] Nola, he says, is "really leading her life as a man, in control,"[4] which she has every right to do. At the end of the film, the character looks into the camera and explains simply, "It's about control. My body. My mind. Who's gonna own it, them or me?"

Lee placed a high value on realism in this film, as he tries to do in all his projects. "I just want to present black people as I know them," he told *Jet* magazine, "as I know they haven't been portrayed in Hollywood."[5] This is important to Lee because he believes that the movie industry tends to show African-American people in superficial and stereotyped ways. Much of the time, it doesn't show them at all. "Another reason I did this film was because there are hardly any films about black people."[6]

From the start, Lee knew that money would be a problem. The New York State Council on the Arts allowed him to apply the $18,000 grant that he had received for *Messenger* to this new film. The American Film Institute, however, took back its grant. He did manage to raise $4,000 from private investors, but he would need much more.

Lee knew that the big movie studios would not be interested in this odd little film that they felt would not appeal to a large audience. "If I had gone to Hollywood for the money for this film with an all-black cast," he says, "they'd have said, 'Forget it.' I always knew I was going to have to do it on my own."[7]

That is why he calls his production company Forty Acres and a Mule Filmworks. At the end of the Civil War, the government had promised to make available to each former slave a forty-acre parcel of land and a mule to help farm it. But the promise was broken and they received nothing. To Lee, the name is a constant reminder that, as an African-American filmmaker, he can rely on no one but himself.

Lee hated to begin shooting without having raised all the money he needed. After all, just one year before, a lack of money had sunk his dream and he had ended up broke and depressed. But he couldn't wait any longer. In July of 1985 he started production on *She's Gotta Have It*. He had about $13,000 left in the bank and that would not last very long.

It was a no-frills job, fast and cheap all the way. Lee managed to get his cast and crew to accept "deferred payment." In other words, they agreed to wait to get paid.

Lee's production company, Forty Acres and a Mule Filmworks, is located in this former firehouse in Brooklyn, New York.

The production literally existed from day to day, and each day was an anxiety-driven adventure—"guerrilla filmmaking," as Lee likes to call it. At night, when that day's shooting was over, Monty Ross, the film's production supervisor, would call or write everybody he and Lee knew and beg them to send money. Those who were not turned off by their bad experience with *Messenger* agreed to invest in the project.

Around midday, Ross would rush home to look in his mailbox, hoping that some checks had come. "I remember a couple of times," Lee recalls, "when Monty, during the shoot, would leave the set and I would fill out the deposit slip and he would run to the bank and deposit the checks. So that's the kind of duress we made this film under."[8]

Most of the scenes in *She's Gotta Have It* take place in what was supposed to be Nola's loft. It was actually an attic above a Brooklyn restaurant. It was a typical sweltering New York summer, and the windows didn't open. Even when the hot movie lights were turned off, the atmosphere was stifling. "It must have been 104 degrees up there," Lee explains. "When it's so hot, people drink a lot and I remember saying, 'Don't throw away the bottles.' "[9] The soda bottle deposits helped pay for film.

The shooting was completed in an incredible twelve days, and Lee immersed himself in the postproduction phase of the project. He edited the film in his own small apartment, using a rented editing machine that was

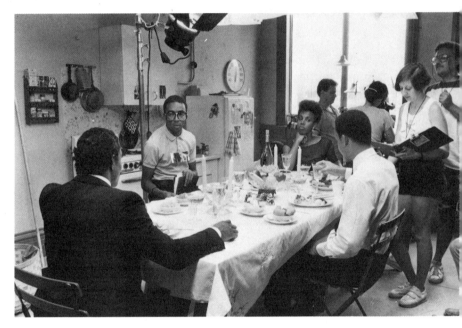

Lee meets with the cast and crew of *She's Gotta Have It*. Everyone involved worked long hours and finished shooting the film in just twelve days.

wedged between his bed and his huge record collection. *She's Gotta Have It* occupied his every waking moment. "Everything was wrapped up in getting this film made,"[10] Spike admits.

All the while Lee was, as he wrote in his diary, "flat broke. STARVIN' like MARVIN."[11] His rent was overdue, his phone and power were turned off. Creditors breathed down his neck. The rented soundtrack machine was taken away. He owed so much money to the film processing lab that it threatened to auction off the movie's negative if he didn't pay up.

Lee persevered. He managed to come up with enough money to complete the movie by screening the unfinished film for audiences of prospective investors. In the end, *She's Gotta Have It* was made on a budget of $175,000, an incredibly low cost in this day of multimillion-dollar motion pictures. Many television commercials cost more to produce.

It was released in the spring of 1986 and premiered at the San Francisco Film Festival in March. Lee invited a number of movie distribution companies to attend this debut. He hoped that if the film were a hit at the festival, one of these companies might be interested in distributing it.

The theater was packed. *She's Gotta Have It* was about to make its world premiere. Suddenly, that section of San Francisco was hit with a blackout. Lee sat on the dark stage, answered questions from the audience, and prayed for the power to come on again. A half hour later the blackout ended and the showing resumed. Afterwards, a bidding war began among the distributors. They could see that *She's Gotta Have It* would be a profitable product.

In May, at France's prestigious Cannes Film Festival, Spike Lee won the *Prix de Jeunesse,* the Young Director's Award. The career of "Spike Lee, Filmmaker" got its first big boost. After Cannes, Lee decided to sell the worldwide distribution rights to Island Pictures, one of the smaller companies. He liked its imaginative marketing ideas, such as selling T-shirts, posters, and buttons at movie theaters.

Lee was glad to have a distributor, but he balked at Island's plan to promote the movie as a comedy, even though there are plenty of laughs in *She's Gotta Have It.* Like many creative artists, Lee uses humor to call attention to serious subjects. Looking back on his work, he once commented, "None of my movies are comedies."[12]

Comedy or not, when the film opened in August, movie reviewers praised Lee's directing debut. David Denby of *New York* magazine enjoyed the film's "loose and easy" feeling, and its "pleasantly open-ended structure."[13] The *New York Times'* critic, Vincent Canby, announced, "here's a filmmaker who possesses not only a point of view and something to say . . . but also the drive to get movies made, which is exceptionally rare when attached to talent."[14]

Pauline Kael, in a generally positive review for *The New Yorker*, also declared that the twenty-nine-year-old Spike Lee showed something very rare, " 'a film sense.' It's an instinct about how to make a movie move," she explained. "When a director has it it's as if nature intended him to make movies."[15]

Certainly the film had flaws—the tiny budget and the first-time director's inexperience saw to that. Still, most reviewers decided to look past these limitations. They heralded the debut of an important new filmmaking talent. And in January 1987, the Los Angeles film critics honored Lee with their New Generation Award.

She's Gotta Have It also was a big hit at the box office. During its first week, the film sold $1.8 million in ticket sales. Over its entire theatrical release, it grossed between $7 and $8 million—an astounding return on its poverty-level budget.

Lee was especially pleased that both black and white moviegoers had come to see his film. "When I wrote the script," he admits, "I had a black audience in mind. But that's not to say that nobody else can enjoy it."[16]

Spike Lee had accomplished a rare feat for a first-time filmmaker. His inexpensive, quirky movie was liked both by audiences and critics, and on top of that, it made money. The Hollywood establishment could not help but be impressed by this young maverick.

5

"Wake Up!"

Part of his mission, Spike Lee continually emphasizes, is to make movies for and about African-American people. His first film, *She's Gotta Have It* proved that it could be done. "This film," Lee observed in an interview with *Ebony* magazine, "stands as an example that we can make our own films, and we don't need a million dollars to do it."[1]

Of course, it doesn't hurt to have a million dollars, if you can get it. When Lee began work on his second film, *School Daze,* Island Pictures guaranteed him a budget of between $1 and $2 million. This was not a huge amount by Hollywood's standards—at the time, the average film budget was around $12 to $14 million.

The project was not free of financial anxieties, however. Lee's plans included location shooting, a large-scale musical soundtrack, sixty speaking parts, and between 3,000 and 4,000 extras. His budget rose to nearly $4 million and Island began to get worried. "I remember them specifically saying," he recalls," 'Spike, this might be too big a leap for you. Why don't you just do a $1-million film, and do *School Daze* later?' "[2]

Then, late one Monday night in January of 1987, Lee was awakened by a call from an Island executive. The company had decided that the picture was just too expensive, and it wanted out of the deal. It seemed like *She's Gotta Have It* all over again.

This time, though, Lee would not have to beg for contributions from family, friends, and strangers. The box-office success of his debut picture had opened doors for the twenty-nine-year-old director. The next morning, Tuesday, Lee started calling the big Hollywood studios. That afternoon he traveled to Manhattan and delivered a copy of the script to David Picker, the president of Columbia Pictures. On Wednesday, Lee and Columbia cut a deal, and on Thursday he flew to Los Angeles for meetings. Columbia would give him the budget he needed—$6 million.

At first, Lee naturally was bitter about being dropped by Island. He soon got over that feeling and came to think of it as a real break for him. "In retrospect," Lee reflects, "Island's dropping me was the best thing that could have happened. *School Daze* is my arrival in the big leagues, and we needed a major studio."[3]

School Daze deals with a subject that had been on

Lee's mind since his days at Morehouse College. "Light-skin blacks have historically done better in this society," he lamented to *People* magazine. "I want to show that the vestiges of slavery are still with us in the way we think."[4]

White racism, Lee felt, created this kind of color bias within the black race. However, he also blamed many African-American people for valuing light skin color and individual material success over racial pride and solidarity. These sorts of preoccupations, Lee cautioned, are holding back the progress of African Americans as a group. "We just want to show that all that stuff needs to be put aside," he says, explaining the message of his film, "[and] that we as black people need to work together."[5]

School Daze takes place at "Mission College," a fictitious all-black institution similar to the one Lee himself attended. The school is divided into two hostile cliques—the lighter skinned, more success-oriented children of affluent African-American families and the darker, more socially conscious students. Lee predicted that many people would be "highly upset" with his new movie.[6] He was right.

In early 1987 Lee began shooting the film on the campus of his alma mater, Morehouse College. After three weeks, though, the college refused to allow him to continue working there. Even though Lee wanted to make a realistic film about the black college experience, and more importantly, the problem of color prejudice among African Americans, the school issued a statement: "Morehouse does not want to be associated with the movie for what it might imply."[7]

According to Lee, the college's president, Hugh Morris Gloster, "thought this would be a negative portrayal of black colleges." Gloster admitted that he was afraid parents "would judge the school on what they see in this film."[8] Spike Lee was forced to pack up and leave Morehouse. And he was told that all of the film shot there—three weeks worth of work—would have to be removed from the film. Luckily, he was able to restart the project at nearby Atlanta University, an all-black graduate school.

When *School Daze* was released in February, 1988, Lee braced himself. He knew that after his stunningly successful filmmaking debut, expectations for this movie would be very high. He would have to prove that *She's Gotta Have It* was not just a fluke. "On your first film," he was quoted in the *New York Times* magazine as saying, "people will fall all over you. With your second film, the audience and critics will be laying for you. They're ready to put you to the firing squad."[9]

On the whole, the critics were lukewarm in their reviews of *School Daze*. David Denby, of *New York* magazine, called the film "messed-up, [and] insanely ambitious," and asserted that "Lee can't seem to find the right tone."[10] He was especially critical of the musical numbers, as was the *New York Times'* Janet Maslin. She

Actors on the set of *School Daze*. Lee (far right) played Half-Pint, a fraternity pledge, in the film.

wrote that they were "overlong" and "more like pointless entertainment than anything else." Maslin, however, did admit that, despite the movie's flaws, it "is still the work of a brave, original, and prodigious talent."[11]

Roger Ebert, the influential film critic of the *Chicago Sun-Times,* was more favorable. He did feel, though, that the picture had a few loose ends, and that some scenes didn't seem to fit. Still, Ebert called Lee's use of musical sequences "an inspiration," and praised him for confronting "issues that aren't talked about in the movies these days."[12]

Lee knew that by taking on these issues he risked upsetting many African Americans. Like the officials at Morehouse, they might feel that he was airing their dirty linen in public. "They're going to be using that tired line," Lee warned, " 'Why do you want white folks to know about what we're doing?' "[13]

His fears were well-founded. The United Negro College Fund cancelled plans for a benefit premiere. (Nevertheless, Lee, Columbia Pictures, and its parent companies, Coca-Cola USA and the Coca-Cola Company, each donated $25,000 to the Fund.) Willi Wear, the firm started by the late African-American fashion designer, Willi Smith, dropped its plans for a screening party, even though Smith had designed dresses that were used in the film. The *Amsterdam News,* a New York African-American newspaper, charged that *School Daze* had set black people back 200 years.

Spike Lee defended himself against those who felt such matters are best swept under the rug. "I didn't show all this divisiveness just to say we're divided," he maintained. The point was to present the problem and get African Americans talking about it. Maybe then, he hoped, they might begin working together and overcome the divisions. "How can you correct anything," Lee added, "if you don't at least acknowledge the problem and try to work on it?"[14]

School Daze ends on a serious and passionate note. Dap, the outspoken student, rings the large college bell and calls the students out of their beds—"Waaake uuuup!" he shouts. They assemble in the courtyard outside their dorms, the dark-skinned and the light, the activists and the apathetic. Finally, Dap's antagonist, Julian, the fraternity leader, joins him. They look into the camera and Dap speaks directly to the audience in the theater: "Please, wake up."

All the criticisms and controversy had little effect on moviegoers. They made *School Daze* a box-office hit. For a movie to make a profit, it must earn double what it cost to produce. Spike Lee's second film grossed $5 million in its first two weeks and eventually earned three times its original budget. It was Columbia Pictures' most profitable film of 1988, even though the studio gave the movie very little advertising support. "There was no TV advertising," Lee complains, "no subway ads, no ads in black magazines. It was successful because of word of mouth."[15]

Lee's first two movies, *She's Gotta Have It* and *School Daze,* illustrate his two-part mission as a filmmaker. First, he wants to make realistic movies about real African-American people. "I'm tired about people who know nothing about us defining our lives," he complains.[16]

And so, the characters in these films are funny, smart, creative, interesting people. They lead complex lives. They have problems that they are trying to resolve. They have dreams and fears. But most of all, they are *black.* Through them, Lee overturns the stereotyped ways that Hollywood has portrayed African Americans. "We want to show," he often says, "that we're not all hanging around the ghetto shooting up, selling crack."[17]

Second, Lee wants to make movies that stimulate and provoke the audience. "Any time a film gets people talking," he said, "that's a step in the right direction."[18] His first two films got plenty of people talking. *School Daze* even caused some real controversy. Spike Lee, however, welcomed this uproar. After all, the whole idea was to make the audience think—to wake them up.

6

"Trying to
Hone My Craft"

"Filmmaking has to be one of the hardest endeavors known to man," Spike Lee once told interviewer Pete Hamill. "Just to make *a* film. To make a *good* film is really like a miracle."[1]

Like most movie directors, Spike Lee has his own way of working. On the set he is thoughtful and silent, completely focused on the job, and he gets impatient when interrupted. Once the camera begins rolling and the actors begin acting, Lee seems to dissolve into the background. Actor Larry Fishburne, who played Dap in *School Daze*, observes, "Sometimes Spike has his back turned and his eyes closed. He will just listen."[2]

Many actors want feedback from their director and are a little confused when they don't get it from Lee. "Spike really doesn't communicate verbally with actors a lot," Fishburne continues. "I'll look at him like I'm wondering, 'Hey, am I doing OK?' And he nods."[3] Nevertheless, veteran actor Ossie Davis, who has appeared in many of Lee's films, appreciates the director's unobtrusive style. "His touch is so light you don't even know it's there," Davis notes, "yet it is."[4]

As a filmmaker, Spike Lee knows what he wants, and he works long and hard to achieve it. Still, he does take the ideas of his cast and crew into account. He even lets his actors improvise dialogue in their scenes, something that many directors will not allow.

But in the end, Lee feels, the director must have the final say. "Film is a director's medium," he maintains. "I try to listen to everybody's suggestions, but the final outcome ultimately is going to be my decision."[5] After all, the critics, the public, and the studio hold the director responsible for the success or failure of the movie.

One of the most noticeable characteristics of Spike Lee's films is the number of family members involved in the production. "If you have a talented family," he insists, "you should be shot if you don't use them."[6] So he does use them—father Bill Lee wrote the musical scores for his first four films; sister Joie has acted in his movies; brother David serves as still photographer for Lee's projects; and his aunt, Consuela Lee Moorehead, was assistant music supervisor on *School Daze* and plays the piano in one scene.

It is not easy to work closely with family members, especially when, as the director, you are their "boss." It is normal for actors and directors to have artistic disagreements. If the people involved are brother and sister, like Spike and Joie Lee, the conflicts may seem personal. "A lot of times when I give her direction," he observes about his sister, "she thinks I'm giving it to her as a big brother. But I am the director."[7]

It gets even more difficult when one of your "employees" is also your father, a gifted artist with strong ideas of his own. "It's hard," Lee agrees. "Because he's a perfectionist and a nonconformist, and I love him because he's my father, but he's not the easiest person to work with."[8]

For example, during the production of *She's Gotta Have It,* Bill and Spike Lee had what the director called "a big fight" over some of the music. Bill Lee wanted to compose a jazz piece to introduce the streetwise, "hip-hop" character, Mars Blackmon. "I knew," Lee maintains, "there was no way in the world Mars would listen to the kind of music my father writes."[9] In the end, of course, the director won the argument.

Spike Lee enjoys a strong relationship with both his sister and his father, and their respect for each other as artists goes very deep. It's not always easy, but they do their best to keep creative differences from becoming family arguments.

To a great extent, Lee's casts and crews are like

family. Lee is loyal to his talented co-workers, and he tends to use many of the same people in different films. Actor Giancarlo Esposito, who has appeared in three of Spike's films, believes that this sort of stability helps make good movies. "What's good about working with people you've been with before," he claims, "is that you have a camaraderie instead of a competition."[10]

Co-producer Monty Ross met Lee when they were freshmen at Morehouse and has worked with him on every film since *She's Gotta Have It.* Ross feels that the personal relationship Lee has with most of his key people has helped them develop their skills. "Spike's approach is to treat us like family, not employees," he says, "and each of us is a professional because of this family. You get a chance to really expand your craft with Spike."[11]

Another key element of Spike Lee's films is that he acts in them; he appears as a supporting character. He got the idea while he was working on *She's Gotta Have It.* "I never acted before," Lee explains. "Well, halfway through writing this film, I decided, hey, I should play this role."[12] Since he had such a tiny budget to work with, it was a wise economic decision. He could save money by using one less actor. So, he became Mars Blackmon, the funniest character in the new film.

As a first-time filmmaker, Lee quickly discovered with *She's Gotta Have It* that it is not easy to wear two hats at one time. "The first day it was horrible," he admits, "because I was trying to direct and act. You can't do that."[13] The solution, however, was simple. In scenes where Lee had to act, Ernest Dickerson, his NYU classmate and trusted cinematographer, assumed the role of director.

In his second film, *School Daze*, Lee created for himself the part of Half-Pint, the small fraternity pledge, another comic character. Audiences enjoy and relate to Lee's on-screen appearances, and he takes advantage of this audience-appeal in his dealings with Hollywood. "It's just one more ace in the hole," he notes, "leverage I can use to get my films made, because any time I go to the studios the first thing they ask me is am I going to be in it."[14] So, he continues to appear in his movies, pleasing both the audiences and the studio executives.

Film critic Roger Ebert once remarked that he would like to see Spike Lee in a starring role. Lee, however, does not believe that he could carry an entire film, though. "I don't think I'm really an actor," he told Ebert. "I think the little I do, I do well, and I get out of the way and let the real actors take over."[15] In addition, Lee is concerned that if he spends too much time in front of the camera it will detract from his real work—directing.

To his surprise, Lee's first two movies brought him sudden wealth and fame. "I'm not making movies to become famous," he said in *Jet* magazine shortly after *She's Gotta Have It* appeared, "or become filthy rich or

Lee works with Ernest Dickerson, his trusted cinematographer, on the set of *School Daze*.

to have 10 million beautiful women. I just want to present black people as I know them."[16]

Still, Lee took his newfound success in stride. "I still don't have any furniture," he admitted to *Ebony* magazine a full year after *She's Gotta Have It.* "I still don't have a car. And no, I still don't even have a driver's license. That stuff is not important to me."[17] He continued living in his old neighborhood, "to stay in touch," he told Hamill.[18] He still pedalled around the Brooklyn streets on his bicycle, dressed in his usual baseball cap and sneakers.

Of course, as one of the world's most devoted sports fans, Lee is always ready to take advantage of one fringe benefit of his fame. "The part I like about success is," he explained to Roger Ebert, "I get to go into the locker room after the game. I get to have great seats at the game."[19] Rubbing elbows with sports heroes is, to Spike Lee, better than all the big cars, fancy clothes, and Beverly Hills mansions that his money could buy.

But perhaps the greatest reward, to Lee, is that he is able to work at something that he really enjoys, making movies. "The important thing," he says, "is, I'm doing what makes me happy. Ninety-nine percent of the people in this world go to their grave having worked at a job they hated."[20]

Lee's early triumphs in feature films helped open up other doors for him. In late 1986, he was chosen to direct a music video for the master jazz trumpeter Miles

Davis. Davis had rejected three other directors before his recording company, Warner Brothers, suggested Lee for the job. Since then, he has directed videos for Anita Baker, Branford Marsalis, Public Enemy, Steel Pulse, and Tracy Chapman.

In the spring of 1988, Lee donated his time and talents to make a thirty-second commercial for Rev. Jesse Jackson, who was seeking the Democratic party's presidential nomination. "I wanted to do something," he announced, "to show there are black people who support him." The black and white spot uses strikingly original visual techniques and focuses on Jackson's crusade against drugs. In the ad, the two men try to show that, in the director's words, "drugs are not just pertaining to blacks and Hispanics in the inner city. It affects everybody."[21]

Lee's most famous non-movie projects are his television commercials, particularly the popular series that he created for Nike's Air Jordan basketball shoes. The company's ad writer and producer had seen *She's Gotta Have It*. They got the idea of using Lee not only to direct a commercial, but also to appear in it as Mars Blackmon, the character he played in the film.

Maybe the best part of this job, for Spike Lee, was getting to work and hang out with Chicago Bulls superstar Michael Jordan, who appeared in the ad. "I think he would've done the commercial free, just to meet Michael," one of the advertising men joked. Jordan

Michael Jordan and Spike Lee teamed up for a series of television commercials, including this public service ad urging students to stay in school. Lee both starred in and directed the ads.

also enjoyed meeting Lee. "Spike's fun to be around," he says, "*and* he knows basketball."[22]

The original commercial was so successful that Nike hired Lee to do a series of spots with Jordan. His ads helped move the company past Reebok and Converse, straight to the top of the $5.5-billion sneaker market. Since then, Lee also has directed commercials for Diet Coke and Levi's jeans.

But for Spike Lee, these are only fun, and profitable, diversions from his "real" work—making movies. "I think of the commercials that I do," he observes, "and also the music videos, as exercises that really keep me trying to hone my craft between feature films."[23] So, in 1988, hot on the heels of the release of *School Daze*, Lee began writing his next film, which he titled *Do the Right Thing*.

7

The Right Thing

The script for Spike Lee's new film, *Do the Right Thing,* was inspired by real-life events. The most notorious of these was the murder of a black man by a gang of whites in the Howard Beach section of New York in December of 1986. "Howard Beach gave me the idea, the impetus for the film," Lee explains, "but it's not the Howard Beach story."[1] He also dedicated the film to the families of African Americans who died in a series of New York police brutality cases.

Script in hand, Lee began looking for a studio to produce the film. He knew that Hollywood might balk at his controversial theme—racism. However, he also felt that, as long as his pictures made money, he could find a studio that would let him make his movie, his way. "I have a script, and they know I have final say," he made clear. "If they want to do the film, these things have to be met, or else we don't do it."[2]

Lee did not bother approaching Columbia Pictures with the project. The studio had put so little effort into promoting *School Daze* that, in his view, "going back to Columbia would be suicide."[3] Paramount Pictures was the first studio to read his script. They wanted him to rewrite the explosive climax. Lee refused and moved on.

He didn't have to go too much farther. "I let some people at Universal know about it," he recalls. "They said yes the same weekend Paramount said no. It was that easy, you know?"[4] Universal gave Lee a budget of $6.5 million, and the full creative control upon which he had insisted.

Lee shot the film entirely on location in Brooklyn's Bedford-Stuyvesant neighborhood. He felt that it was important to cement a friendly relationship with the community. Before the shooting began, Lee threw a block party that was attended by a local hero, the then-heavyweight boxing champ Mike Tyson.

He hired local residents to be extras and crew members. He gave away clothing and renovated people's apartments. When it was time to tear down the Korean grocery set that was constructed for the film, he distributed the food. He set up a scholarship program for the local high school. When shooting was completed, Spike Lee could say with pride, "People respected us—who we were and what we were trying to do."[5]

The story takes place in Bedford-Stuyvesant on one sweltering day. Lee wanted the summer heat to be a "character" in the film, interacting with the other characters and affecting the way they behaved. "How does heat affect already-tense race relations in New York City?" he wondered.[6] *Do the Right Thing* attempts to explore that question.

The movie opens with the same words that ended *School Daze*, as the voice of a radio disc jockey is heard getting his listeners out of bed—"Waake uuuup!" This is a key to Spike Lee's message. As in *School Daze*, he wants his audience to wake up to the nature of racism, how it is expressed, how people are affected by it, and how it can erupt when those people finally decide that enough is enough.

Lee's characters are complex and confused individuals, and the situations he creates for them are complicated. "There are no heroes or villains in the film," he maintains.[7] Actor Danny Aiello puts it in a similar way. "Everybody is a jerk," he feels, "and everybody has their moments."[8]

Aiello plays Sal, the Italian pizzeria owner who has an uneasy relationship to the neighborhood. Sal is not a bad person, but he is stubborn and insensitive. He can't understand why one of his black customers, Buggin' Out, is irritated because the "Wall of Fame" in his restaurant includes only pictures of Italian Americans and no African Americans.

Spike Lee cast Danny Aiello as "Sal", the pizzeria owner, in *Do the Right Thing.*

Lee wants the audience to see both characters' points of view. "Buggin' Out rightfully felt that Sal should have the decency to have some black people up on the Wall of Fame," he argues, "since all his income is derived from people in the community who are black or Hispanic. Sal had, to me, a more valid point: This is my pizzeria and I can do what I want."[9] The fact that they cannot resolve this difference leads ultimately to tragedy.

Lee has his biggest role as Mookie, Sal's delivery man. The bright, likeable, but somewhat irresponsible, character represents, Lee explains, "a large portion of the young black males today. He's really just living from day to day without thinking about the future."[10]

At the film's climax, Sal and Mookie collide. When the police kill a young African-American man who was involved in a conflict with Sal, Mookie hurls a garbage can through his employer's plate glass window. This ignites the people in the neighborhood, who then burn down the pizzeria. They have their revenge, but what have they gained by it? Their friend is dead, Sal's business is destroyed, and the neighborhood is now doubly poorer.

The concluding quotations—by Dr. Martin Luther King, Jr. on nonviolence and Malcolm X on self-defense—heighten the movie's open-ended quality. "They both wanted the same thing for black people," Lee maintains. "It's just that they chose very different routes to arrive there."[11] Lee has said many times that he

Spike Lee appeared in his film *Do the Right Thing* as the likeable "Mookie," a pizza delivery person. The film was shot on location in Bedford-Stuyvesant.

leans more toward Malcolm's philosophy. Still, in the film he does not take sides. It is, he feels, up to the audience to choose their own routes, as well.

Some critics gave *Do the Right Thing* strong reviews. Vincent Canby of the *New York Times* called it "a remarkable piece of work," and said that it "is living, breathing, riveting proof of the arrival of an abundantly gifted new talent."[12] He praised almost every aspect of the movie—Lee's writing and directing, Ernest Dickerson's vivid camera work, Wynn Thomas' set design, Bill Lee's music, and the acting of the ensemble cast, especially Danny Aiello and Lee.

Roger Ebert agreed that this was a "very well-made film." Most of all, he commended the realism with which Lee framed the movie's central issue. In Ebert's view, it "comes closer to reflecting the current state of race relations in America than any other movie of our time."[13] At the end of the year, Ebert and his television partner, Gene Siskel of the *Chicago Tribune*, both chose *Do the Right Thing* as the best film of 1989.

But other influential reviewers were not so positive. *New York*'s critic, David Denby, questioned the film's realism. He felt that "Lee's version of a poor neighborhood is considerably sanitized, without rampaging teenagers, muggers, or crack addicts."[14]

Likewise, Richard Corliss of *Time* noted, "On this street there are no crack dealers, hookers, or muggers."[15] He also said that the film "is ultimately false and pernicious," concluding his review with a snide, "Take a hike, Spike."[16] In *Newsweek*, Jack Kroll observed, "Lee's Bed-Stuy omits too many things to justify his claim of reality; most startlingly, there's not a single reference to drugs."[17]

These writers also feared that the film would incite racial violence. Denby warned: "If some audiences go wild, he's partly responsible."[18] Kroll wrote, "this movie is dynamite under every seat. Sadly, the fuse has been lit by a filmmaker tripped up by muddled motives."[19]

Spike Lee and *Do the Right Thing* became one of the hottest stories of the summer of 1989. It jumped out of the entertainment sections and onto the editorial pages. Magazines and newspapers all across the country took turns attacking or defending the filmmaker and his latest work. Joe Klein, then *New York*'s political columnist, predicted that if Spike Lee's "reckless new movie" attracted a large number of African-American viewers, "there's a good chance the message they take from the film will increase racial tensions in the city."[20]

Lee spent most of the summer responding to his critics. On the issue of realism, he argued that although his film takes place in a poor neighborhood, that did not mean that it had to look like a slum. "There's no need to show garbage piled up high and all that other stuff, because not every single block in Bed-Stuy is like that," Lee insisted. His characters did not have much money, but they did have dignity and self-respect. "These are

Spike Lee once again teamed up with friend Ernest Dickerson for the making of *Do the Right Thing*.

hard-working people," he maintained, "and they take pride in their stuff just like everybody else."[21]

He had been hearing, and answering, one question ever since the film's premiere at Cannes in May—why are there no drugs in the movie? "With this film, I could not be sidetracked by another issue," he explained to *Time* magazine. "The larger issue at hand was racism."[22]

Finally, on the subject of whether *Do the Right Thing* might cause violence, Lee told *US News & World Report*, "It wasn't made to incite riots, but to provoke discussion about racism, something people do not want to do." Critics who made that charge, he countered, "think that black youth won't be able to tell what's a movie and what's real life."[23]

The controversy was good publicity, and Lee took advantage of it. ABC News devoted an entire installment of its "Nightline" program to the *Do the Right Thing* debate, and, of course, Lee appeared on it. "It's a very entertaining movie," he said at the close of the show, "everybody should come out and see it, and I think that they should make up their own minds."[24] Apparently, people were doing just that—in its theatrical release, *Do the Right Thing* grossed $27.5 million.

As fall of 1989 approached, it became clear that New York and the rest of the country would survive *Do the Right Thing*. There were no riots. Black audiences did not run out of theaters and attack white people, as some of Lee's critics feared. There was, however, one bitterly ironic incident of racial violence in New York that summer. An African-American man who ventured into the largely Italian section of Bensonhurst in Brooklyn was killed by a white mob.

In March of 1990, when the Academy Award nominations were announced, *Do the Right Thing* was not nominated in the Best Picture category. Lee did get nominated for Best Original Screenplay—but not Best Director—and Danny Aiello was nominated for Best Supporting Actor. Spike admitted that he was disappointed, "but I'm still going to the ceremony and enjoy myself." *Los Angeles Times* film critic Sheila Benson spoke on behalf of his supporters. "Spike, you wuz robbed," she wrote. "Again."[25] At the awards ceremony, neither Danny Aiello nor Spike Lee won the Oscar in their categories.

That spring, Lee found himself immersed in more controversy, not because of his movies this time, but because of his commercials. In cities throughout the United States, people were being robbed, and even killed, for the expensive athletic shoes or satin team jackets they were wearing. In nearly every case, both the victim and the perpetrator were young African-American men.

In an article titled, "Shaddup, I'm Sellin' Out . . . Shaddup," *New York Post* sports columnist Phil Mushnick criticized celebrities like Lee and Michael Jordan whom, Mushnick felt, glamorized these products in commercials geared toward black teenagers. He charged that they were, in some part, responsible for these senseless deaths. "It's murder, gentlemen," he wrote. "No rhyme, no reason, just murder. For sneakers. For jackets. Get it, Spike? Murder."[26]

Lee shot back a reply in the sports daily, *The National.* He accused Mushnick of "thinly veiled racism." He asked why the columnist had criticized only African-American celebrities and ignored white athletes, like Joe Montana and Larry Bird, who also appear in sneaker commercials.

More to the point, Lee argued that there were deeper social causes of the violence and that these have to be addressed. "Let's try to effectively deal with the conditions that make a kid put so much importance on a pair of sneakers, a jacket or gold," he insisted. "These kids feel they have no options, no opportunities."[27]

Getting an education, he felt, is the key. And so, later that year, he directed and appeared with Jordan in a Nike-sponsored public service advertisement that urges their young fans to stay in school.

The previous twelve months had been a difficult and challenging period for Spike Lee. He had faced nearly constant controversy and criticism, and all he had done was make a movie and direct some commercials. He was just trying to do his job, just trying to 'do the right thing.'

8

"Just Trying to Tell a Good Story"

By early 1990, Spike Lee was at work on his next movie, which, he promised, would be very different from the inflammatory *Do the Right Thing*. "It's not an angry or antagonistic film," he said. "Now they'll say I sold out."[1]

He originally intended to call it *A Love Supreme*, after a classic composition by the late jazz saxophonist, John Coltrane. Coltrane's estate objected, so he renamed it *Variations on a Mo' Better Blues*. Lee eventually cut this rather unwieldy title to simply *Mo' Better Blues*.

Like most of his films, the subject matter of *Mo' Better Blues*—jazz and jazz musicians—comes straight out of Lee's observations and experiences. As he was growing up, he saw how his father, jazz bassist Bill Lee, refused to compromise his art. "Everything I know about jazz," he explains, "I know from my father. I saw his integrity, how he was not going to play just any kind of music, no matter how much money he could make."[2]

Lee felt that past Hollywood portrayals of jazz artists were largely negative. He wanted to reverse the stereotype of the jazz musician as an irresponsible, solitary, self-destructive figure. "I wanted to show a man who could make decisions," he maintains, "who had a family life, who wasn't a drug addict or alcoholic."[3]

Lee learned from his father and other musicians that artistic creation is more the result of discipline and hard work than of so-called genius. This was reflected in his movie. "I wanted to show these guys *practicing*," he asserts. "Wynton Marsalis practices six hours a day. It's not just a natural ability."[4]

Mo' Better Blues is the story of a fictional jazz musician, Bleek Gilliam, and his single-minded commitment to his art. "I know what I want—my music," the character declares. "Everything else is secondary." On one level, the film celebrates the talent and creativity of African-American artists, but it also has a deeper message. People who become obsessed with their work, Spike warns, are in danger of losing their perspective and alienating those who are closest to them.

Lee wrote the part of Bleek Gilliam specifically with Denzel Washington in mind. "This film was tailor-made for him," Lee told Roger Ebert. "He is star quality. . . . He is handsome. Plus he can act on top of all that."[5] The role gave Washington a chance to draw upon his many

Denzel Washington and Spike Lee as they appeared in Lees' film *Mo' Better Blues*. Washington played "Bleek Gilliam," a part Lee wrote especially for him.

resources as an actor—drama, romance, even some comedy.

Since Washington is not a musician, Lee hired jazz trumpeter Terence Blanchard to coach the actor so that he would look like he really was playing the instrument. The actual trumpet parts on the film's soundtrack were played by Blanchard, who wrote some music for the film. Saxophonist Branford Marsalis, who is heard on the soundtrack, and Bill Lee also composed some of the music.

Just one year earlier, Spike Lee had thrilled some critics and disturbed others with *Do the Right Thing*. When *Mo' Better Blues* opened in the summer of 1990, most of them were, at best, disappointed. David Ansen wrote in *Newsweek* that the film "rings as hollow as the Hollywood pablum Lee always rejected," and thought that the final section "feels like a commercial for life insurance."[6]

The *New York Times*' reviewer, Caryn James, also found little to praise. She found the movie "so trite in its depiction of artists and so laughable in its stab at romance," and dismissed it as "one long cliché, the kind that might make his most loyal admirers wince and wonder, 'Spike, what happened?' "[7]

Even Roger Ebert of the *Chicago Sun-Times*, one of those loyal admirers, admitted that *Mo' Better Blues* is "a less passionate and angry film than *Do the Right Thing*, and less inspired, too." However, Ebert's review was, on the whole, positive. He concluded with the observation that "the film has a beauty, grace, and energy," and that although it "is not a great film, it's an interesting one, which is almost as rare."[8]

That's all Lee was after, really, to make an interesting movie. As he said to *Essence* magazine shortly before the release of *Mo' Better Blues*, "I'm just trying to tell a good story and make thought-provoking films."[9]

On the day before the premiere of *Mo' Better Blues*, Spike Lee began another, quite different project—his own store, Spike's Joint. Located in a Brooklyn brownstone about a block from his Forty Acres and a Mule Filmworks office, the store specializes in merchandise connected with his films, like posters, T-shirts, caps, and books. Lee always believed that merchandising was essential for promoting his movies, particularly when the studio's advertising budget was small. Now he had an outlet for just that purpose.

Throughout 1990 and into 1991, Lee kept up an exhausting schedule. By the time *Mo' Better Blues* appeared in theaters, he already was casting his next film. Shooting began in mid-August and ran until early November. "We'll be working seven days a week," Lee told Roger Ebert, "just to get it finished in time for the Cannes Film Festival next May." On top of that, there were more Nike and Levi's commercials to direct, an issue of *Spin* magazine to guest-edit, and, "of course, basketball season begins in November."[10]

Lee opened his own store in Brooklyn in 1990. Called Spike's Joint, the store specializes in merchandise connected with Lee's films.

He also produced a feature for Home Box Office (HBO) about then-heavyweight champ Mike Tyson and his flamboyant manager, Don King. Lee believed that the white-dominated sporting press never treated Tyson and King fairly. He decided to give them the chance to tell their side of the story.

The film was shown on cable TV before Tyson's successful title defense against Alex Stewart in December of 1990. According to *Sports Illustrated*'s Rick Reilly, "not only was the documentary longer than the fight, but it also was far more interesting."[11] Lee lost $7,000 on the project, but he felt it was worth it, especially after it won two Emmy Awards.

And as if all this were not enough to keep him busy, in January of 1991, Spike Lee started his own record company, Forty Acres and a Mule Musicworks. Through it, he plans to produce recordings in a broad spectrum of musical styles—jazz, rhythm and blues, soul, funk, hip-hop, world beat, and more. By the end of 1992, Lee's label had released albums by the keyboard/vocal duo State of Art, Senegalese bandleader Youssou N'Dour, and R&B/pop singer Lonette McKee.

In his new film, *Jungle Fever*, Lee tackled an explosive subject—a romance between an African-American man and an Italian-American woman. "It's [about] the two neighborhoods they're from, Harlem and Bensonhurst," he explained in *Rolling Stone*, "and the boundaries that are crossed, and what happens to

Jungle Fever told the story of a romance between an African-American man (played by Wesley Snipes) and an Italian-American woman (played by Annabella Sciorra). Veteran actors Ossie Davis and Ruby Dee portrayed Snipes' parents.

you when you cross those boundaries, how you're looked upon by friends, family, and the neighborhoods they come from."[12]

Like *Do the Right Thing*, Lee's story was inspired by a brutal, racially motivated murder in New York. In the summer of 1989, a young black man, Yusef Hawkins, was killed by a white mob in the Bensonhurst section of Brooklyn, a largely Italian area. "Yusef was killed," Lee maintains, "because they thought he was the black boyfriend of one of the girls in the neighborhood."[13] *Jungle Fever*, however, does not tell the story of the Hawkins case. Rather, it attempts to examine the kind of prejudice that makes this sort of violence possible.

Lee made a point of shooting many of the scenes in the same neighborhood where Hawkins was killed. One night, he received three bomb threats. He and actor Wesley Snipes had rocks thrown at them, and cameraman Ernest Dickerson actually was hit by a rock. Headlines in the New York tabloids read, "Cops Guard Spike Lee." The set became a circus of reporters and TV crews. But despite it all, the movie got made. Lee wrote that, "we were well received. Going in, I thought it was gonna be much worse."[14]

Two things were significantly different in the production of *Jungle Fever*. For the first time, neither Joie nor Bill Lee were involved in the project. "Joie felt it was time to start to establish her own identity," Lee explains. He offered her a small part anyway, "just to

Spike Lee with Wesley Snipes in a scene from *Jungle Fever*. While shooting the film on location in Brooklyn, the cast and crew received bomb threats and had rocks thrown at them.

Lee confers with Annabella Sciorra, the actress who co-starred with Wesley Snipes in *Jungle Fever*.

keep her working," but she turned it down. "She made the right choice," he believes.[15]

It was a different matter with Bill Lee. "His scores keep getting better and better," the director felt, "but it was also getting harder for us to work together. So, we both mutually agreed to take a time-out."[16] Lee came up with an excellent substitute to write the music for *Jungle Fever*—Stevie Wonder. But he does hope to work with his father again in the future.

Although the central theme of Lee's new film was race, it also addressed the subject of drugs. Two years earlier, many reviewers criticized *Do the Right Thing* because Lee had avoided the drug issue in it. At that time he had argued that, "Drugs is such a massive subject, it just can't be dealt with effectively as a subplot."[17]

By *Jungle Fever*, however, Lee, having matured as a filmmaker, was able to do just that. He created the role of Gator, the crack-addicted brother of one of the main characters, the successful architect, Flipper. Through them, Lee showed how drugs can split a family beyond repair, until tragedy is inevitable.

When the film was shown at Cannes in May 1991, Vincent Canby declared in The *New York Times* that it was the "clearly popular favorite for the *Palme d'Or*, the festival's top prize."[18] However, the Cannes judges did not see it the same way and awarded the grand prize to another film. The only recognition that *Jungle Fever* received was a special award for best supporting performance given to Samuel L. Jackson for his chilling portrayal of the crackhead brother. Lee was disappointed. "We wuz robbed," was his only comment, but he said it with a smile.

When the film opened in June, Canby announced, "With *Jungle Fever*, Spike Lee joins the ranks of our best."[19] He was not alone in his opinion. Even some reviewers who did not like *Do the Right Thing* praised *Jungle Fever*. For example, Richard Corliss of *Time* found the film both "brazen" and "assured," and said, "As it spirals into the underworld of hatred and despair, *Jungle Fever* kicks into movie overdrive." He particularly praised the "primal power" of the scenes in the crack den.[20]

Likewise, *Newsweek*'s Jack Kroll, another of the earlier film's harshest critics, wrote "The 34-year-old filmmaker's best movie, it raises more issues than any American film in a very long time."[21] It also became Spike's most profitable movie, ticket sales totalling $32 million in theaters throughout the United States.

That summer, Lee told Pete Hamill in *Esquire* that he was somewhat surprised to find that people thought of him as a spokesperson on political and social questions. "I'm not trying to be a leader," he insisted, "I'm just a filmmaker."[22] But one thing was clear—Spike Lee had emerged as a leader among American filmmakers.

9

"Whose Malcolm Is It Anyway?"

Spike Lee never seems to rest—he just goes straight from one major project into the next, with a hefty handful of minor ones on the side. "My grandmother thinks I might have a heart attack or something," he joked to Roger Ebert.[1] *Jungle Fever* was barely finished when Lee began work on perhaps the most challenging assignment of his career—a film biography of the militant African-American leader of the early 1960s, Malcolm X.

Every previous attempt to produce a movie about the life of Malcolm X has failed. Two years after Malcolm X's death in 1965, producer Marvin Worth purchased the film rights to *The Autobiography of Malcolm X.* The late novelist James Baldwin began a screenplay in early 1967, but he abandoned the project a year later with the script only two-thirds done. Another writer, Arnold Perl, finished it. Since then, Worth went through four more writers and three directors, and still no film was made.

In 1990, Worth and Warner Brothers hired Canadian director Norman Jewison. When Lee heard that a white filmmaker was selected for the job he was upset. "That disturbs me deeply, gravely," he complained. "It's wrong with a capital W. Blacks have to control these films."[2]

His problem with Jewison was neither personal nor professional. "I respect what he does," Lee made clear. "I saw *In the Heat of the Night, A Soldier's Story.* . . . But I think a black man is more qualified."[3] It was an unpopular position to take, but he felt that he could back it up. Citing the *Godfather* trilogy, Lee argued, "Italian-American [director] Francis Coppola brought nuances a non-Italian wouldn't have gotten."[4] And so, he believed that an African-American director would have insights into Malcolm's life that a white filmmaker, however talented, would not.

Jewison started work, but bowed out in November of 1990, not so much because of Lee's criticisms, but because of his own frustration. "If I knew how to do it, I would move heaven and high water tomorrow to do it. The man's an enigma to me," the exasperated filmmaker admitted. The door was now open for Lee. "I know Spike Lee wants to get involved and, at the moment, I would encourage him to do it," Jewison added graciously, "because the film should be made."[5]

At this point, Worth decided that the film "needed a black director. . . . It was insurmountable any other way."[6] Spike Lee signed a deal with Warner Brothers in early 1991 and began rewriting the original Baldwin-Perl script. To portray Malcolm, he cast his *Mo' Better Blues* star, the powerful actor Denzel Washington. (Interestingly, Jewison also chose Washington for the title role.) By September, Lee was ready to begin shooting *Malcolm X.*

Ironically, just as Lee had criticized the selection of Jewison, there were those who criticized the choice of Lee. In early August, over a month before shooting started, a group called The United Front to Preserve the Legacy of Malcolm X held a protest rally in Harlem. Two hundred people attended. The group's spokesperson, poet-playwright-activist Amiri Baraka, accused Lee of making films that perpetuate racial stereotypes, and declared, "We will not let Malcolm X's life be trashed."[7]

Lee was baffled—Malcolm X was his hero. Why did Baraka and his followers think his film was going to trash Malcolm? They had not even read his script. However, he tried to be responsive to the protesters. "I understand the concerns," Lee admits, "because I went through it myself with Norman Jewison."[8] He said that he would welcome and listen to advice.

Nevertheless, this was his project and he would not allow the film to be made by committee. He remained

Denzel Washington was once again cast by Lee in 1991, this time to portray Malcolm X in Lee's controversial film.

confident that his skill and experience were equal to the task. "All I can say is: I was the director, I rewrote the script by James Baldwin and Arnold Perl, and I will take full responsibility. . . . This is the Malcolm that I see."[9]

Lee also resented the way Baraka seemed to have set himself up as the sole keeper of Malcolm's legacy. "Whose Malcolm is it anyway?" he wrote in response to the protestors. "Malcolm belongs to everyone. I reserve my right as an artist to pursue my own vision of the man."[10]

Lee's vision was not exactly what the studio originally had in mind, however. "It's an epic story," he insisted. "It could run 3 hours and 10 minutes. I told Warner there was no way it would be 2 hours 10." Of course, to make a film of that length and scope costs money, and Lee maintained, "I don't intend to come up short."[11]

However, Warner Brothers' production president, Mark Canton, foresaw "a relatively modest, average budget, less than $20 million."[12] Lee wanted $30 million, but settled for $28 million, the largest budget he had ever had. As usual, he insisted on retaining full creative control over the project. "I'm gonna make the film I'm gonna make," he assured his audience. "This is definitely not a time to change that, not on a film as important as this."[13]

Clearly, Spike Lee's *Malcolm X* was an ambitious undertaking. His script required a great deal of location work, not just in New York's Harlem, but also in Africa and Arabia, where Malcolm traveled during the last year of his life. This all proved very expensive, and in early March of 1992 the press reported that Lee had exceeded his budget, by "a few million," and that the bond company was about to take over financial control of the filming.

Whenever a studio decides to make a major motion picture, it purchases what is known as a "completion bond" as a kind of insurance policy. The bond company guarantees to the banks and the distributors that in the event of unforeseen problems the film will be completed. If the film goes over budget, as did *Malcolm X*, the bond company routinely assumes financial control of the project and can refuse to approve further expenditures.

In Hollywood, a budget of $28 million is just about average, overruns are quite common, and bond companies often take financial control of films. A spokesperson for the bond company could not understand all the publicity in this instance. "Our interest is only to ensure that the work continues and gets done on time," he noted.[14]

Perhaps if it had been any other filmmaker and any other film, this would have been a nonstory. Spike Lee, however, always attracts attention—often unwanted— and *Malcolm X* had generated its share of controversy, both before and after Lee got the assignment. So the story became newsworthy, and it raised a reasonable question: Would Spike Lee be able to retain his usual "full creative control" with someone else managing the purse strings?

Lee decided to take matters into his own hands. He contacted a number of African-American celebrities and asked them to help bail him out. On May 19, 1992, Malcolm X's birthday, he called a press conference in Harlem to thank Bill Cosby, Magic Johnson, Oprah Winfrey, Prince, among others, for donating the extra $6 million he needed to complete the film.

Spike Lee's *Malcolm X*—starring Denzel Washington and featuring Ernest Dickerson's cinematography, Wynn Thomas' set designs, and a musical score by Terence Blanchard—opened on November 18, 1992. In three hours and twenty-one minutes of vivid sights and sounds it tracks Malcolm's life through its many stages—criminal, convict, religious convert, minister-organizer for the Nation of Islam, and ultimately, an independent, militant black leader. Lee's film reaches its tragic climax when Malcolm X is assassinated while delivering a speech.

But the movie does not end on a sad note. Rather, Lee constructs a powerful tribute to this fallen hero: the screen fills with images of the real Malcolm X; actor Ossie Davis reads the eulogy that he delivered at Malcolm's funeral; African-American school children stand up and declare, "I am Malcolm X!"; and black South African leader Nelson Mandela speaks about

Malcolm's message. In this way, Lee links Malcolm with the struggle for racial justice that still is going on around the world today.

Leading film critics praised *Malcolm X*. Roger Ebert, on the *Siskel and Ebert* television program, called it "a triumph," "a masterpiece," and "one of the most absorbing, entertaining, and challenging film biographies I've seen." His TV colleague, Gene Siskel, agreed. Siskel also felt that the expensive location work, which had caused the film to run over budget, was worth the added cost. "It's very exciting," he observed, "to see a whole life that spans, literally, the globe."[15]

David Denby, the critic for *New York* magazine, has been no great fan of Spike Lee's work. "I squirmed through Lee's recent films, *Mo' Better Blues* and *Jungle Fever*," he stated, point blank. But Denby admitted that he enjoyed *Malcolm X*. "Most of it," he wrote, "is rock solid—stirring, emotionally challenging, and even funny."[16]

However, Richard Corliss of *Time* felt that after all the pre-release hype, the film itself was a letdown— "high-minded mediocrity" and "tepid melodrama," as he put it. "The big surprise about *Malcolm X*," Coliss remarked, "is how ordinary it it."[17] Still, most reviewers echoed *Newsweek's* David Ansen, who accounced, "Lee and company have performed a powerful service: they have brought Malcolm X very much to life again, both as man and myth."[18]

Malcolm X scored a solid hit with audiences, as well. It opened strongly, selling $10.5 million in tickets by the end of its first weekend. But despite the strong reviews, attendance soon began to level off, for a number of reasons.

First, Warner Brothers did only minimal advertising for the film. Of course, Lee, as usual, generated plenty of free publicity in the months prior to its release. But the studio suspended its television advertisements for *Malcolm X* just a week after it opened, and did not resume the commercials until a month later. Then, a flood of holiday releases cut into *Malcolm X*'s potential box office. Movie-goers preferred to spend their dollars on lightweight, less demanding fare, like the hugely popular *Home Alone 2.*

Finally, *Malcolm X*'s longer than normal running time—three hours and twenty-one minutes—almost certainly reduced its box office receipts. It simply could not be shown as many times in one day as the more common ninety minute to two-hour movies. As a result, fewer tickets could be sold in any given theater.

In addition, Warner Brothers' research found that three-quarters of the movie's audience was twenty-five or older. It seemed that younger people, either because of the length or the serious subject matter, had decided that *Malcolm X* was not a "date film." But whatever the reason, teenagers with X's on their T-shirts and baseball caps were not flocking to see Lee's film, as he had hoped.

Still, *Malcolm X* was not a flop. By the end of 1992 its earnings approached $40 million and continued to climb. Its March 1993 European opening would bring in more money—although not for Warner Brothers, who sold the foreign rights to the film, which it later regretted. The eventual home video release also promised substantial earnings.

And the film did find a sizeable audience among African Americans *over twenty-five*. A spokesman for a chain of 300 theaters in California estimated that blacks made up between 70 and 80 percent of the audience at most locations. That information must have pleased Lee. "We want black people to be inspired and really apply what [Malcolm X] said to their personal lives," he has stated, many times. "And if we listened to what he said, we wouldn't be in the state we're in."[19]

A *Black* Filmmaker

In February 1992, while he was still working on *Malcolm X,* Lee tackled a new and very different task. The African-American studies department at Harvard University gave him a one-semester appointment to teach a class called "Contemporary African-American Cinema." The course surveyed the various ways that black people have been portrayed on film since the 1960s, and examined how these changing images reflect American society.

Lee selected sixty students for the course based on essays they had submitted prior to the semester. "They're going to have to work," he told *Jet,* "they're going to have to write papers, see films. No backsliding, no skating in this class."[1]

Every Wednesday, films chosen by Lee were screened for the class. (Among these was his first movie, *She's*

Gotta Have It.) On the following Friday, he took time out from his shooting schedule to discuss that week's movie with them. "He's one of the most effective discussion leaders I've had," said one of Lee's students. "He lets people speak their minds and brings up insightful things that only a black filmmaker could say."[2]

Black Filmmaker—Lee has ambivalent feelings about the term. On the one hand, he believes that it implies a somewhat lesser status. "Black people are not thought of as equals," he argues, "therefore, you have a qualifying word like the 'black' director."[3] He has a valid point—Steven Spielberg or Martin Scorsese, for example are almost never referred to as "white" directors.

At the same time, Lee has decided, "I'm not going to spend one iota of energy denying the fact that I'm a black director. I think it's useless."[4] And so, he is committed to making serious, realistic movies that focus on the experiences and concerns of African Americans. "I just try and draw upon the great culture we have as a people," he explains, "from music, novels, the streets."[5]

Whether Lee likes the term or not, since the start of the 1990s, a new crop of young African-American filmmakers has arrived on the scene. In 1991 alone, of the nearly 140 films distributed by the major companies, 19 dealt with African-American themes—more than in the entire preceding decade. Among the most heralded of these were Mario Van Peebles' *New Jack City,* John Singleton's *Boyz N the Hood,* and *Straight Out of*

Brooklyn by nineteen-year-old Matty Rich. Lee's longtime cinematographer, Ernest Dickerson, made his directing debut in early 1992 with *Juice.*

"Spike put this trend in vogue," notes Mark Canton of Warner Brothers. "His talent opened the door for others." Van Peebles agrees. "If it weren't for Spike," he insists, "I wouldn't be here."[6] *She's Gotta Have It* taught Hollywood two important lessons: first, that African Americans could make movies, and second, that movies by and about African Americans could make money. The rest of Lee's films—with even bigger profits—reinforced this message.

The studios, eager to duplicate Spike Lee's successes, began giving small budgets to, and reaping huge returns from, young African-American directors. For example, *New Jack City* was made for just $8.5 million and grossed more than $47 million. *Boyz N the Hood,* which was made for only $6 million, took in over $57 million. "All these films mean," Lee observes, "is that Hollywood can make a dollar off them. Black films will be made as long as they make money."[7]

Spike Lee's influence on this black new wave is clear. Like him, they are trying to use their movies to make hard-hitting social statements. "If you make a film," Singleton has remarked, "you have a responsibility to say something socially relevant."[8]

Many of these films focus on a common theme—the urban ghetto and the struggles facing the young

African-American men who live there. In a sense, they are like variations on *Do the Right Thing* and *Jungle Fever*. Noticing this, Lee urges his younger colleagues to work from a broader range of themes, plots, and characters. "We seem to be in a rut," he told an African-American film conference at Yale University.[9]

Lee also advises these up-and-coming filmmakers to study and learn their craft, as he did. "A lot of these guys making films today," he observes, "they're proud to say, 'I didn't go to film school, I never made a film before.' Most of the time it ends up looking exactly like that."[10]

If these young, energetic upstarts do begin to stretch their talents and visions, they also may push Lee to make even more innovative films himself. However, Lee warns that unless African-American directors start making more original and better-crafted films, the public will grow bored with their movies—*all* of their movies, including his. If that happens, Hollywood could lose interest in them.

By 1992, danger signs began to emerge. Even though overall, the studios released the same number of movies as in the previous year, there were only half as many new films by black directors as in 1991. (Some Hollywood insiders predicted that this number would pick up somewhat in 1993.) The young African-American filmmakers, Spike Lee included, began to realize that in order to continue making pictures, they must keep earning high profits for the studios.

Interviewers often ask Lee what place he hopes to occupy in film history. Early in his career, he told *Ebony* magazine that he would like to be thought of "as a great filmmaker who left behind 20 or 30 very good films."[11]

In a 1992 *New York Times* interview he added to that wish. "I want to be remembered," he said, "for honest, true portrayals of "[African Americans] and for bringing our great richness to the screen."[12] Having made six movies in seven years, each one focusing on some aspect of African-American life, Spike Lee is well on the road to achieving these goals. The journey ahead promises to be long and bright.

Chronology

1957—Born in Atlanta, Georgia on March 20.

1959—Family moves to Brooklyn, New York.

1975—Attends Morehouse College in Atlanta.
-1979

1979—Enrolls in master's degree program at New York University's film school.

1983—Student film, *Joe's Bed-Stuy Barbershop: We Cut Heads*, wins student Academy Award.

1986—First feature film, *She's Gotta Have It*, debuts; wins *Prix de Jeunesse* at the Cannes Film Festival; is chosen to direct Miles Davis music video.

1987—Directs and appears in first of a series of Nike commercials with Michael Jordan.

1988—*School Daze* released; directs presidential campaign ad for Rev. Jesse Jackson.

1989—*Do the Right Thing* released.

1990—*Mo' Better Blues* released; directs HBO documentary about boxer Mike Tyson.

1991—Starts own record label, Forty Acres and a Mule Musicworks; *Jungle Fever* released.

1992—Teaches African-American film course at Harvard University; *Malcolm X* released.

The Films of Spike Lee

She's Gotta Have It (1986)

School Daze (1988)

Do the Right Thing (1989)

Mo' Better Blues (1990)

Jungle Fever (1991)

Malcolm X (1992)

Chapter Notes

Chapter 1

1. David Handleman, "Insight to Riot: Director Spike Lee's 'Do the Right Thing' Takes a Provocative Look at Race Relations," *Rolling Stone*, April 13–27, 1989, p. 107.

2. Jeannie Williams, "Will 'Right Thing' Hit at Wrong Time?" *USA Today*, May 22, 1989, p. 4D.

3. Ibid.

4. Handleman, p. 107.

5. Williams.

6. Handleman, p. 107.

7. Ibid., p. 174.

8. Ibid., p. 175.

Chapter 2

1. B. Little, "Brooklyn's Baby Mogul, Spike Lee, Finds the Freedom He's Gotta Have," *People*, October 13, 1986, p. 70.

2. Rick Reilly, "He's Gotta Pitch It," *Sports Illustrated*, May 27, 1991, p. 82.

3. Ibid., p. 84.

4. Bill Hasson, "Jazz on Location: Filmmaker Spike Lee," *Jazz Times*, January 1990, p. 16.

5. Roger Ebert, *Roger Ebert's Movie Home Companion: 1992 Edition* (Kansas City: Andrews and McMeel, 1991), p. 714.

6. Elvis Mitchell, "Spike Lee," *Playboy*, July 1991.

7. David Ansen, "The 'Vision' Thing," *Newsweek*, October 2, 1989, p. 37.

8. Ebert, p. 714.

9. Spike Lee and David Lee, *Five for Five: The Films of Spike Lee* (New York: Stewart, Tabori & Chang, 1991), p. 12.

10. Peggy Orenstein, "Spike's Riot," *Mother Jones*, September 1989, p. 34.

11. Reilly, p. 84.

12. Trudy S. Moore, "Spike Lee, Producer, Director, Star, Discusses Making of Film, 'She's Gotta Have It,' " *Jet*, November 10, 1986, p. 56.

13. Reilly, p. 84.

14. Ibid., p. 82.

15. Orenstein, p. 35.

Chapter 3

1. Elvis Mitchell, "Spike Lee," *Playboy*, July 1991.

2. Peggy Orenstein, "Spike's Riot," *Mother Jones*, September 1989, p. 34.

3. Mitchell.

4. Bill Hasson, "Jazz on Location: Filmmaker Spike Lee," *Jazz Times*, January 1990, p. 16.

5. Pamela Johnson, "The Making of 'School Daze': Behind the Scenes," *Essence*, February 1988, p. 130.

6. Bonnie Allen, "The Making of 'School Daze': Talking with Spike," *Essence*, February 1988, p. 130.

7. Stuart Mieher, "Spike Lee's Gotta Have It," *New York Times Magazine*, August 9, 1987, p. 39.

8. Orenstein, p. 35.

9. Larry Rohter, "Spike Lee Makes His Movie," *New York Times*, August 10, 1986, sec. 2, p. 18.

10. Spike Lee and David Lee, *Five for Five: The Films of Spike Lee* (New York: Stewart, Tabori & Chang, 1991), p. 13.

11. Ibid.

12. Ibid.

13. Rick Reilly, "He's Gotta Pitch It," *Sports Illustrated*, May 27, 1991, p. 84.

Chapter 4

1. David Frichette, "Spike Lee's Declaration of Independence," *Black Enterprise*, December 1989, p. 56.

2. Larry Rohter, "Spike Lee Makes His Movie," *New York Times*, August 10, 1986, sec. 2, p. 14.

3. Trudy S. Moore, "Spike Lee, Producer, Director, Star, Discusses Making of Film, 'She's Gotta Have It,'" *Jet*, November 10, 1986, p. 55.

4. Rohter, p. 14.

5. Moore, p. 56.

6. Marlaine Glicksman, "Lee Way," *Film Comment*, September-October 1986, p. 48.

7. B. Little, "Brooklyn's Baby Mogul, Spike Lee, Finds the Freedom He's Gotta Have," *People*, October 13, 1986, p. 67.

8. Glicksman, pp. 47–48.

9. Elvis Mitchell, "Spike Lee," *Playboy*, July 1991.

10. Ibid.

11. Rick Reilly, "He's Gotta Pitch It," *Sports Illustrated*, May 27, 1991, p. 84.

12. Peggy Orenstein, "Spike's Riot," *Mother Jones*, September 1989, p. 43.

13. David Denby, "Roughing It," *New York*, August 18, 1986, p. 59.

14. Vincent Canby, "Films for Viewers Who Think for Themselves," *New York Times*, September 7, 1986, sec. 2, p. 28.

15. Pauline Kael, "The Current Cinema: Bodies," *New Yorker*, October 6, 1986, p. 129.

16. Rohter, p. 18.

Chapter 5

1. "He's Gotta Have It," *Ebony*, January 1987, p. 44.

2. Pamela Johnson, "The Making of 'School Daze': Behind the Scenes," *Essence*, February 1988, p. 52.

3. Spike Lee, "Class Act," *American Film*, January-February 1988, p. 59.

4. B. Little, "Brooklyn's Baby Mogul, Spike Lee, Finds the Freedom He's Gotta Have," *People*, October 13, 1986, p. 70.

5. "He's Gotta Have It," p. 48.

6. Ibid.

7. "Spike Lee Filming Banned at Alma Mater in Atlanta," *Jet*, March 11, 1987, p. 55.

8. Stuart Mieher, "Spike Lee's Gotta Have It," *New York Times Magazine*. August 9, 1987, p. 26.

9. Ibid., p. 41.

10. David Denby, "A Color Line," *New York*, February 29, 1988, p. 117.

11. Janet Maslin, "Film: 'School Daze,'" *New York Times*, February 12, 1988, sec. 3, p. 11.

12. Roger Ebert, *Roger Ebert's Movie Home Companion: 1992 Edition* (Kansas City: Andrews and McMeel, 1991), p. 525.

13. Bonnie Allen, "The Making of 'School Daze': Talking with Spike," *Essence*, February 1988, p. 130.

14. Ibid.

15. Peggy Orenstein, "Spike's Riot," *Mother Jones*, September 1989, p. 43.

16. Mieher, p. 26.

17. Ibid., p. 39.

18. Allen, p. 130.

Chapter 6

1. Pete Hamill, "Spike Lee Takes No Prisoners," *Esquire*, August 1991, p. 26.

2. Stuart Mieher, "Spike Lee's Gotta Have It," *New York Times Magazine*. August 9, 1987, p. 41.

3. Ibid.

4. Jeannie McDowell, "He's Got to Have It His Way," *Time*, July 17, 1989, p. 94.

5. Marlaine Glicksman, "Lee Way." *Film Comment*, September-October 1986, p. 51.

6. Ibid., p. 46.

7. "Spike Lee Admits to Some Squabbles with Sister on 'Mo' Better Blues' Set," *Jet*, August 8, 1990, p. 57.

8. Ibid., p. 51.

9. Greg Tate, "Burn, Baby, Burn," *Premiere*, August 1989, p. 35.

10. Samuel G. Freedman, "Spike Lee and the 'Slavery' of the Blues," *New York Times*, July 29, 1990, sec. 2, p. 9.

11. Ibid.

12. Glicksman, p. 48.

13. Ibid.

14. Tate, p. 82.

15. Roger Ebert, *Roger Ebert's Movie Home Companion: 1992 Edition* (Kansas City: Andrews and McMeel, 1991), pp. 714–715.

16. Trudy S. Moore, "Spike Lee, Producer, Director, Star, Discusses Making of Film, 'She's Gotta Have It,'" *Jet*, November 10, 1986, p. 56.

17. "Waking Up Rich and Famous," *Ebony*, September 1987, p. 42.

18. Hamill, p. 28.

19. Ebert, p. 714.

20. Ibid., pp. 713–714.

21. "Spike Lee Films Ad for Jackson Campaign to Show His Support," *Jet*, May 2, 1988, p. 9.

22. Rick Reilly, "He's Gotta Pitch It," *Sports Illustrated*, May 27, 1991, p. 77.

23. Marcy Magiera, "Lee: Black Films Get Less Support," *Advertising Age*, April 1, 1991.

Chapter 7

1. Greg Tate, "Burn, Baby, Burn," *Premiere*, August 1989, p. 81.

2. Jeannie McDowell, "He's Got to Have It His Way," *Time*, July 17, 1989, p. 94.

3. Peggy Orenstein, "Spike's Riot," *Mother Jones*, September 1989, p. 45.

4. Tate, p. 85.

5. Ibid., p. 82.

6. Ibid., p. 81.

7. Ibid.

8. Susan Spillman, "Lee's Film Is Unsettling, Provocative," *USA Today*, June 30, 1989, p. 2A.

9. David Breskin, "Spike Lee: The Rolling Stone Interview," *Rolling Stone*, July 11–25, 1991, p. 64.

10. Tate, p. 82.

11. Breskin, p. 66.

12. Vincent Canby, "Spike Lee Tackles Racism in 'Do the Right Thing,'" *New York Times*, June 30, 1989, sec. 1, p. 11.

13. Roger Ebert, *Roger Ebert's Movie Home Companion: 1992 Edition* (Kansas City: Andrews and McMeel, 1991), p. 162.

14. David Denby, "He's Gotta Have It," *New York*, June 26, 1989, pp. 53–54.

15. Richard Corliss, "Hot Time in Bed-Stuy Tonight," *Time*, July 3, 1989, p. 62.

16. Ibid.

17. Jack Kroll, "The Fuse Has Been Lit," *Newsweek*, July 3, 1989, pp. 64–65.

18. Denby, p. 54.

19. Kroll, p. 64.

20. Joe Klein, "Spiked?" *New York*, June 26, 1989, p. 14.

21. Marlaine Glicksman, "Spike Lee's Bed-Stuy Barbecue," *Film Comment*, July-August 1989, p. 16.

22. Christopher Dickey, with Peter McKillipp, "That's the Truth, Ruth," *Newsweek*, p. 66.

23. Alvin P. Sanoff, "Doing the Controversial Thing," *US News & World Report*, July 10, 1989, p. 51.

24. Transcript of "Nightline," ABC-TV, July 6, 1989 (New York, Journal Graphics, 1989), p. 9.

25. "Freeman, Washington Get Oscar Nods, Lee Snubbed," *Jet*, March 5, 1990, pp. 54–55.

26. Rick Telander, "Senseless," *Sports Illustrated*, May 14, 1990, p. 44.

27. Ibid.

Chapter 8

1. David Ansen, "The 'Vision' Thing," *Newsweek*, October 2, 1989, p. 37.

2. Samuel G. Freedman, "Spike Lee and the 'Slavery' of the Blues," *New York Times*, July 29, 1990, p. 9.

3. Ibid.

4. Ibid.

5. Roger Ebert, *Roger Ebert's Movie Home Companion: 1992 Edition* (Kansas City: Andrews and McMeel, 1991), p. 713.

6. David Ansen, "Spike Lee Almost Blows It," *Newsweek*, August 6, 1990, p. 62.

7. Caryn James, "Spike Lee's Middle Class Jazz Musician," *New York Times*, August 3, 1990, sec. 3, p. 1.

8. Ebert, pp. 387–388.

9. Jill Nelson, "Mo' Better Spike," *Essence*, August 1990, p. 106.

10. Ebert, p. 714.

11. Rick Reilly, "He's Gotta Pitch It," *Sports Illustrated*, May 27, 1991, p. 85.

12. David Breskin, "Spike Lee: The Rolling Stone Interview," *Rolling Stone*, July 11–25, 1991, p. 71.

13. Jack Kroll, "Spiking a Fever," *Newsweek*, June 10, 1991, p. 45.

14. Spike Lee and David Lee, *Five for Five: The Films of Spike Lee* (New York: Stewart, Tabori & Chang, 1991), p. 16.

15. Ibid., p. 11.

16. Ibid.

17. Marlaine Glicksman, "Spike Lee's Bed-Stuy Barbecue," *Film Comment*, July-August 1989, p. 16.

18. Vincent Canby, "'Jungle Fever' Sweeps Cannes," *New York Times*, May 17, 1991, sec. 3, p. 1.

19. Vincent Canby, "Spike Lee's Comedy of Sorrows," *New York Times*, June 7, 1991, sec. 3, p. 10.

20. Richard Corliss, "Boyz of New Black City," *Time*, June 17, 1991, p. 68.

21. Kroll, p. 44.

22. Pete Hamill, "Spike Lee Takes No Prisoners," *Esquire*, August 1991, p. 26.

Chapter 9

1. Roger Ebert, *Roger Ebert's Movie Home Companion: 1992 Edition* (Kansas City: Andrews and McMeel, 1991), p. 714.

2. Anne Thompson, "Malcolm, Let's Do Lunch," *Mother Jones*, July-August 1991, pp. 29, 57.

3. Elvis Mitchell, "Spike Lee," *Playboy*, July 1991.

4. Thompson, p. 57.

5. Ibid., p. 29.

6. David Ansen, "The Battle for Malcolm X," *Newsweek*, August 26, 1991, p. 54.

7. Evelyn Nieves, "Malcolm X: Firestorm Over Film Script," *New York Times*, August 9, 1991, sec. 2, p. 1.

8. Nieves, p. 3.

9. Henry Louis Gates, Jr., "Just Whose 'Malcolm' Is It, Anyway?" *New York Times*, May 31, 1992, sec. 2, p. 13.

10. Spike Lee, "The Director Takes on His Detractors," *Newsweek*, August 26, 1991, p. 53.

11. Thompson, p. 57.

12. Ibid.

13. Ibid.

14. "Lee's 'Malcolm X' Film Exceeds $27 Million Budget," *Jet*, March 2, 1992, p. 60.

15. *Siskel and Ebert*, syndicated television program, November 13, 1992.

16. David Denby, "Washington and Lee," *New York*, November 25, 1992, pp. 70–71.

17. Richard Corliss, "The Elevation of Malcolm X," *Time*, November 23, 1992, p. 65.

18. David Ansen, "From Sinner to Martyr: A Man of Many Faces," *Newsweek*, November 16, 1992, p. 74.

19. Andy Jones, "Spike Lee Primes the 'X' Pump," *New York Newsday*, August 24, 1992.

Chapter 10

1. "Spike Lee Teaches Film Class at Harvard University," *Jet*, February 24, 1992, p. 22.

2. "Cinema a la Spike Lee in a Curious Setting," *New York Times*, March 1, 1992, sec. 1, p. 43.

3. Roger Ebert, *Roger Ebert's Movie Home Companion: 1992 Edition* (Kansas City: Andrews and McMeel, 1991) p. 715.

4. Ibid.

5. Jill Nelson, "Mo' Better Spike," *Essence*, August 1990, p. 106.

6. Richard Corliss, "Boyz of New Black City," *Time*, June 17, 1991, p. 65.

7. Ibid., p. 68.

8. Ibid.

9. "Lee: Gotta Have Better Films," *New York Newsday*, April 13, 1992.

10. Henry Louis Gates, Jr., "Just Whose 'Malcolm' Is It, Anyway?" *New York Times*, May 31, 1992, p. 16.

11. "He's Gotta Have It," p. 48.

12. Gates, p. 16.

Further Reading

Breskin, David. "Spike Lee: The Rolling Stone Interview." *Rolling Stone*, July 11–25, 1991.

Corliss, Richard. "Boyz of New Black City." *Time*, June 17, 1991.

Ebert, Roger. *Roger Ebert's Movie Home Companion: 1992 Edition*. Kansas City: Andrews and McMeel, 1991.

Gates, Henry Louis, Jr. "Just Whose 'Malcolm' Is It Anyway?" *New York Times*, May 31, 1992.

Glicksman, Marlaine. "Lee Way." *Film Comment*, September-October, 1986.

Handleman, David. "Insight to Riot: Director Spike Lee's 'Do the Right Thing' Takes a Provocative Look at Race Relations." *Rolling Stone*, July 13-27, 1989.

Lee, Spike and David Lee. *Five for Five: The Films of Spike Lee*. New York: Stewart, Tabori & Chang, 1991.

McDowell, Jeannie. "He's Got to Have It His Way." *Time*, July 17, 1989.

Mieher, Stuart. "Spike Lee's Gotta Have It." *New York Times Magazine*, August 9, 1987.

Orenstein, Peggy. "Spike's Riot." *Mother Jones*, September 1989.

Reilly, Rick. "He's Gotta Pitch It." *Sports Illustrated*, May 27, 1991.

Tate, Greg. "Burn, Baby, Burn," *Premiere*, August 1989.

Thompson, Anne. "Malcolm, Let's Do Lunch." *Mother Jones*, July-August, 1991.

Wiley, Ralph. "Great Xpectations." *Premiere*, November 1992.

Index

110